# Hollow Bones

Poems on Grief, Illness,
Mental Health and Healing

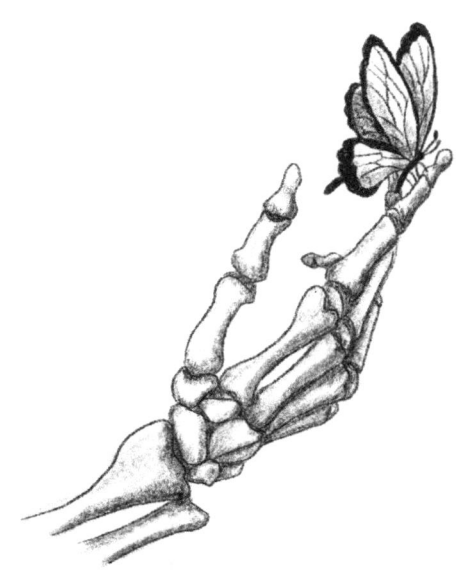

Written & Illustrated
by Freya O'Brien

Copyright © 2025 by Freya O'Brien

All rights reserved. No part of this publication may be reproduced, distributed or transmitted in any form or by any means, including photocopying, recording, or other electronic or mechanical methods, without prior written permission from the publisher, except in the case of brief quotations embodied in critical reviews and other non-commercial uses permitted by copyright law.

First Printing, 2025

ISBN-13: 978-1-7397933-0-2

# content note

before you read

this book contains themes that may be triggering or distressing to some readers, including:

- grief and loss
- death of a parent
- chronic illness and medical trauma
- mental health struggles (including anxiety, depression, and suicidal thoughts)
- emotional abuse and gendered violence

while healing is central to this collection, it is explored through raw, personal experiences.

if you are in a sensitive place,
please take care when reading.

skip when you need to.
breathe when you need to.
you are not alone.

# to the one still standing

*hollow bones* was written in fragments:
on sleepless nights, in hospital waiting
rooms, in the abyss of heartbreak.

it began as a way to survive.

these poems were not written
with polish in mind,
but with feeling.

they are messy,
aching,
and honest.

they sit with fear,
with grief,
and with all the things we are taught
to hide.

if you have felt hollow,
if you have been unravelled,
if you have fought to live in a world
that doesn't see your pain

i hope these words find you.

and that,
even in silence,
you feel heard.

thank you for reading.
thank you for surviving.

– freya

# contents

| | |
|---|---|
| hollow ribs | 9 |
| weathered bones | 37 |
| clenched fists | 53 |
| blurry eyes | 67 |
| whittled mind | 97 |
| quiet soles | 127 |

# hollow ribs

grief echoes loudest
in the spaces
we never thought
would be
empty

# things left unsaid

my dad reads the newspaper
as if it's the
well of life
while my mum
struggles
to hold onto hers

his coldness is a shadow
consuming the room
engulfing us
in things left
unsaid

## do something

i want to scream
to shout
to do something
anything
but my limbs remain locked in place

there is no air in this room

the walls are closing in
tightening

like the fist
digging moons
into my palms

and i am consumed by the silence
that breaks me

# monitors

hospital machines become
as familiar
as my own heartbeat

*beep*
*beep*
*beep*

nurses' eyeless smiles
turn nightmarish

*beep*
*beep*
*beep*

my mum's laughter
goes quiet

*beep*
*beep*
*beep*

breath
is the only sound left

*beep*

    *beep*

       *beep*

          my mum's hand
            goes cold


      **silence**

## once more

the hospital loomed
haunting
imposing

dread
sank into my bones

fluorescent lights
buzzed like flies
over still bodies

i held my breath
as if grief
were contagious

each beeping monitor
a countdown

each hallway
an echo
of something lost

i walked slowly
as if my footsteps
might call her back

i'd give anything
to see her
once more

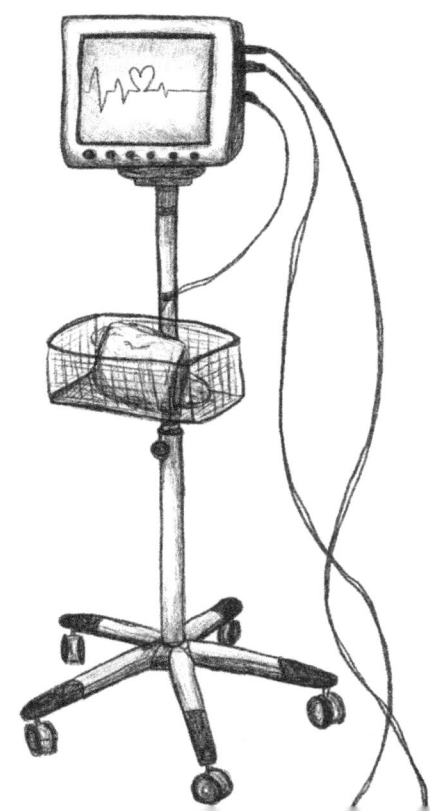

## naive

i thought i knew heartbreak
*how naive was i*

i thought i knew loss
*how naive was i*

i thought i knew the weight
of my soul
*how naive was i*

i thought i knew myself
and my mind
*how*
*naive*
*was*
*i*

# daughter

i am my mother's daughter

her passion for helping others
her quiet creativity
her rounded laugh

i am her softness
her resilience
her legacy

it's a lot
of weight
to bear
for a small child

# a silent undoing

i didn't break loudly

no scream
no shatter
no final breath of flame

just a stitch at first

then the seams
when she went cold
along with my heart

another thread pulled
when i forgot
what joy used to sound like

when silence felt heavier
than the noise ever did

i retreated into that void
i followed directions
nodded at the right times

slowly forgetting
how to speak

until one morning
i looked in the mirror
and saw
no fabric

just wild
    uncut seams

# words

*"keep going"*
*"stay strong"*
*"be positive"*
are empty words
others blindly say

they don't understand
the sheer strength it takes
just to
get through
the day

# borrowed eyes

if i could
i would borrow someone's eyes

i would push them into
my hollow skull
and watch my grey world
turn vibrant

i would see the hope
i would see the smiles
i would see the safety
and whittle away time
for a while

of course
when it came to giving them back
i would
but they would be forever changed
by this suffocating darkness

which no one else can see

# tick tock

grief is quiet
and unyielding

a silent metronome
*tick tock*
*tick tock*
*tick tock*

a hollow frame
void of all life

to a gut punch
shocking
and unrelenting

there's no timeline
no roadmap
no instruction guide

just shifting feet
never knowing
when it will beat again

grief doesn't get better with time
it just changes shape

or
maybe
it's us who change
becoming one with
*shadow*

# mermaid

you called me
your little mermaid
when we swam

before the world cracked open

underwater
you weren't sick
and i wasn't afraid

i don't remember much
just the feel of your hand
as we drifted
weightless
in chlorinated light

grief is tidal
it pulls me back to that pool
where you smiled
and i believed
in magic

# wishes

i could have
a thousand birthday candles
a thousand wishes on stars
a thousand genies or witches

but none of that would matter

because
the only thing i want
is you

# supermarket cake

we used to bake cakes
on birthdays
flour in our hair
icing on our smiles
laughter rising with the batter

now
my pantry is empty
the kitchen is clean
the oven cold

supermarket sponge
invades my mouth
too sickly sweet

the taste of absence

i try to swallow
but it sticks
to the roof of my mouth
refusing to be consumed

and then
i crumble

the grief
is in the aftertaste

no amount of sugar
can cover it

# small things

you live in the small things now

paintbrushes flecked with vivid colour
daisies and meadow flowers

in your favourite places
which have become mine

in the sound of laughter
music and rhyme

in sugar cubes
in woods with tall trees

in the smell of chlorine
and buzzing bees

in morning birdsong
and robins nests

in quiet beginnings
and gentle rest

you live in stillness
in the spaces between

in all the soft moments
and all that has been

and though you are gone
you are never far

i carry you with me
inside my heart

# apple tree

i used to spend hours
playing outside with my sister
dressing up dolls
having bee tea parties
and digging in the dirt

all while the little apple tree
my mum had planted
sat quietly in the shade

when she passed
i sat by the knee-high tree
and hoped it would grow

but it never did

at least
not whilst we lived there

## i am

i am my mother's silent battle
i am my father's stubborn will
i am my sister's wild ambition
i am my best friend's quiet hope
i am my acquaintance's false laugh
i am my stranger's fleeting smile

i am a mosaic
pieced from every soul i've met
however brief
or dark

# lighthouse

she was
a creator
a sculptor
a maker

she crafted joy
with her hands

she laughed gold
baked smiles
and sewed nostalgia
into memory

she painted colour
and canvas
over cancer's dark

until it became
a shadow in the corner
cowering
from her immense light

and
although she didn't win the war

she was
the fiercest warrior
i've ever known

a lighthouse
that still shines
long after she's gone

## ashes

when we scattered
my mum's ashes
into the sea

a bellowing breeze
carried them
far
into the pencil-lined horizon

after years
in hospital beds
i hope she
finally felt

free

# weathered bones

pain settles
into our lives
like dust on a windowsill
only seen
when the light dares

## wild thing

just as i almost feel whole
it starts again

the breaking
the dragging
the weight with no name

i patch myself
with sleep
with silence
with small joys
that don't quite stick

people say it gets better
but *better* is a slippery
wild thing
that refuses to be held

still
i go on
not with hope
just in refusal
to disappear

# safe

you never think to question
how safe your body is
until it happens to you

one day you are living
a normal life
the next
you're in hospital
or more like a zoo

you are poked
and prodded
and sent on your way

*claiming you're cured*

even though
you know
you'll never be okay

# duck

i fight to live every day
a struggle no one sees

like a duck paddling
furiously
underwater

and yet
i appear to glide with ease

# lifeline

my hands may be withered
but yours
are unwavering
as they hold mine

my veins may be bruised
like ink spills

i may be tired
and weary

but you
being here
makes me feel
slightly more
alive

# five pence

i have five pence to spend today
there isn't much i can buy

others have thousands of pounds
while i can barely get by

they spend and spend
with glee
never running out

every time they go to sleep
they don't have to doubt

but this isn't about money
not in the literal sense

i'm talking about my energy
and how mine feels so spent

i charge
and charge
with all my might

but
i stay in the red zone
no matter
how hard
i fight

## weathered

i wake
already tired
the day presses
before it begins

my limbs slow
like weathered branches

my pain
forced into silence
because others
don't want to hear
my cries

how can i hope
when i have nothing left?

i've spent years
hoping
fighting for good
trying to dream
being brave

and
nothing's
changed

this is the shape
of my life
not loud
just worn
and breaking

maybe i'll sink
into hopelessness
for a while
and breathe in
the moon and stars

maybe it's time
i leave the sun
and make my home
in the dark

i am up all night anyway

# ward life

white
starched sheets
air-con breezes
machine beeps
coughs
and sneezes

questionable food
except the jello
nurses
doctors
and voices that bellow

a second home
but not by choice

a scary way
to lose one's voice

# laundry

shock
horror
rinse
re*peat*

stuck in the devil's
laundry cycle

# prison of flesh

my body
is a stranger

a prison
one of a kind

a life sentence

there's no key
or door to find

no escape
from this defective model
which others say
is fine

i wonder
if they experienced it
whether they would
lose their mind

## coffin

i have rested with dracula
for far too long

his night-crawling tendencies
have rubbed off on me

i no longer enjoy
the brightness of day

it's too unforgiving
highlighting the wrong

so
i lament
in my cushioned coffin

painstakingly designed

destined for burial
*alive*

# reluctant

i am the reluctant writer of my life

every twist
an unbendable turn

every plot line
full of holes

every idea
eventually blocked

and yet
i cannot
set down
my pen

# bedside routine

whilst the days blur
into one

the beeping machines
become
morning roosters

the IVs are my coffee

medication leaflets
my newspaper

but nurses' smiles
offering mugs of tea
wake me
from this perpetual
liminal world

and
tether me
to reality

# clenched fists

when no one listens
even a whisper
becomes a scream

## echoes

*"who are you?*
*who are you?*
*who are you?"*

i don't know anymore

but who are you?

where were you
when i was drowning
in my silence

when i was suffocated
by endless darkness

if i'm selfish
then maybe
you were never a good friend

and maybe
you don't know me
after all

## vindictive

your eyes are dulled
by your sharpened knives
blinding you
to anything
but the scent
of blood

your vindictiveness
devours you

cell by cell

and now
it's all
that's left

# bloody words

*"your tests were normal"*
*"shouldn't you be better now?"*
*"it's been going on for years"*

i bathe in your bloody words
until i emerge
red
angry
*raw*

if i could
i'd suffocate these words
from your uttering lips

# frankenstein

am i frankenstein
or his monster

a grave atrocity?

the creator of my own demise
the bearer of an ugly heart
or the one who's
misunderstood?

# blue and red

you were draped in blue
a veil of sadness
quiet and demure

i failed to see
your insides burning red
i hugged you
and my skin caught fire

you laughed at me instead

# burning

my childhood stalks me

a gas only i can see
biting
gnawing
burning

i retreat from its fiery tongue
that leaves no visible wounds

*"Why so jumpy?"*

how
do i get others
to *see?*

## inferno

i burn
hollow words as timber
empty promises as fuel
dirty looks as ignition
silence as my pull

i try to contain my anger
but it burns me instead

and all i'm left with
is shouting in my head

# earthquake

i quake
i shake
i am an earthquake

turning everything to dust
as i try
not to break

*"you are a coward"*

anger replaces fear
and temperance draws near
if you think you can do better
take my life

*here*

# ghost stories

am i cursed for surviving

forever cast as the villain
and never truly seen

a ghost among the living
alone in this crowded world

wearing a crown of shame
stitched from whispers
of a story
i couldn't tell

## you are

you are
the label on my sweater
the condensation on my table
the whir of electricity
the crooked
useless staple

you are
the shrill of a kettle
the umbrella-less storm
a white hair on a black coat
the damp
suffocating warmth

you are nothing more
than annoyance in every way

a rapture of boredom

you won't matter
past today

**within**

you buried yourself
in the hairs on my neck
my shallow lungs
and the goosebumps
on my skin

you turned my blood
to black tar
my stomach to steel
my eyes to roses

while you broke my spirit
from within

# kindling

whilst my head is burning
like wildfire
lapping at my skin
leaving raw
peeling blisters behind

i try to stay calm

i will not let your poker tongue
stoke my flames

i will not let your goading words
become my fuel

i try to remain small
candle-like

a single flame flickering

even if i do
waft a little smoke

# blurry eyes

the world blurs
when you've cried
too long

# almost

i was walking my dog
and i felt safe
i had walked this route a million times

i didn't see the man
coming up behind me

but as soon as he saw my dog
he halted
turned
and walked away

i thought that was the end of it
but it wasn't

i saw him everywhere

outside shops
in doorways
and passing cars

always watching

a lurking shadow
that clung to mine

after i left my hometown
he asked around after me

who knows
what would have happened
if i had
*stayed*

# sculpture

i am not a male
therefore
i am destined to live
the life of a sculpture

      admired

        and

          touched

        yet expected

       to stay

   silent

as they turn my blueness
into gold

# sharks

it's not all men
and yet
if you were surrounded by sharks
would you not be afraid?

would you not watch
their jaws
their speed
their strength
even if they ignored your blood
and swam on by?

and still
some days
i trust a shark
more than a man

because a shark
wouldn't *desecrate* my body

even after i'm gone

## siren

my fear is a siren
luring me lovingly
into the deep

i sink willingly
into the great abyss
letting go of the air
that once sustained me

now
i lie stagnant
on the ocean floor
where no fish
or currents pass

a suffocating existence

an eternal life
not lived

## muted

excitement has lost her voice
her cries go unheard
while anxiety wails
like a relentless banshee

in their battle
your lungs are not your own
they shallowly wheeze

your body is not your own
clenched tight in fear

your mind is not your own
lost deeper each time

in the what-ifs
instead of
what will be

# plummeting

i am the eagle
tumbling to the ground

yet fear won't release me

unyielding

as we both plummet
to our deaths

# puppet

fear settles into my bones
forming a tomb

before i know it
she holds the strings
and my body
isn't my own

i'm pulled away
from what i want
locked in a cowardly prison

all i want
is to rip her out
but my hands
won't listen
to reason

# restless waters

i am sea glass and saltwater
the ebb and flow of tender tides
stirred by the ache of time

i am white horses galloping
to their demise
their death inescapable
outside reason or rhyme

i am the weight of restless waters
saturated with memory
the suffocating sea foam
the siren's weeping history

i am trapped in the abyss of emotion
in waters that never cease
a barrage of quiet
beneath the sea of
silent screams

## venom

fear is a poison
racing through my veins

burning
raging
foaming

until all that's left
is thick sludge

it is relentless
and raw

devouring me
second by second
until
i
break

# curdled

my thoughts curdle
in sadness and fear
emitting quite the stink
to those who draw near

they waft their hands
and lift their noses
at my unsightly mind

don't they see
i too
want to leave
this stink behind?

but i've been pickled
*unintentionally*
for far
too
long

# jack

they turn the handle
and wait
for the pop

i shoot up
eyes wide
mouth open
screaming inside

but they only hear music

and laugh
as they shut the lid

## funny bone

oh where
oh where
is my funny bone
it's not where it should be

i look and search
with all my might
but i still can't find my glee

it's not in my arm
leg
fingers
or toes

all i'm left with
is counting
my heartaches
and woes

# smoke and shadow

the street lamps yawned
the sun forgot to rise
the clock stopped ticking
the stars closed their eyes

the baker burned a dozen loaves
the morning rooster dozed
we tripped on cracked pavements
bullies began to boast

the world started to crumble
draped in night's hued cloak
as we relied on candles to navigate
through glaring daggers
and smoke

# hourglass

my thoughts run
like sand
gliding through
my mind's hourglass
towards their death

escaping
the cage
of my lips
only to whisper
to deaf ears

their destined downfall

# wingless

i fall

effortlessly

toward my impending death

hands empty
relenting into silence
wings turned to dust

# white horses

i am the white horses
dying along the shore

galloping with all my might
to be smashed into oblivion

and yet
i am destined

                to rise



                          and break

                                for eternity

# the fall & rise

my wings are shredded
my bones are broken
my mind is sobbing

i could give up in this moment
and sink
into the
comforting
dark
abyss

but i can't
no
i won't

instead i'll beat my battered wings
and keep aiming for the sky

even if i fall
i will keep trying
until i finally
fly *(again)*

# picking up the pieces

i am a broken plate
shattered
and
scattered

i cut my hands
as i collect my shards
one
by
one

my bloodied hands
cry out

but i keep going

because one day
i will be whole again

# uncertainty

uncertainty
snuffs out my life
steals my breath
squashes my hope
and all i'm left with
is my inevitable death

is this all life is
and all it will be?

a never-ending wave
of change

a never-ending
torment

until i make my home
in its waters

but how do i do that?
if only i knew
*how*

## cages

i'm made from chicken wire
rusted nails
and beaten boards

there's no flesh
blood
or bone left

just an old coop
and my lonely mind

others still see a mirage
of the old me

a whisper of skin
of teeth
and tongue

but they're illusioned too
trapped in their own
twisted cages

the only difference is

i can see mine

# uniform

tired mind
blurred eyes
weary feet
hungry flies

words twisted
lips forlorn
a world burns
in uniform

a mad cycle
of endless decay
while people
go about
their day

# tempest

when will it end

life's
ferocious
relentless
tempest
of a rollercoaster

it doesn't follow
the tracks
laid bare

instead
it lurches
violently
in all directions

as the operator
yields the *illusion*
of control

# sharp

pens scratching
taps dripping
fridges whirring
cutlery scraping
train whistles piercing
cars blaring

a calamity
of senseless noise
in a music-less
razor-edged
world

# inward

i fade
in fluorescent light
television chatter
and the seams of my couch

i shrink
behind closed doors
forgetting
how to be a person
how to move
how to think

my body
holds its breath
as if stillness might save me

but still
the world
presses in

and i
have nowhere left to go
but *inward*

# hollow bones

my hollow bones
drag along the floor
*scratch*
*scratch*
*scratch*

my weary heart
crashes in my chest
*thump*
*thump*
*thump*

my racing mind spins
a kaleidoscope of thoughts
*stop*
*stop*
*stop*

i don't know who i am anymore
who am i?
who am i?
who *am i...*

## dishes

i washed the dishes
without needing music
without needing distraction

just water
and the clink of ceramic
and my hands moving
without shaking

the window was open
and a breeze came in
carrying nothing
but the scent of lavender

for a moment
i forgot to be sad

and when i remembered
it didn't hurt as much

# whittled mind

healing is the silence
between one breath
and the next

# sticky silence

honey bees
buzz in my mind

a ferocious noise
drowning out others
drowning out the world
drowning out myself

until there is nothing left
but sticky honey
oozing from my ears

# hubris

when i was six
i wanted to swim
to the deepest depths
of the ocean
and float
at the bottom of it all

when i was sixteen
i wanted to race to the sun
to feel her fiery rays
lick my skin

now i know
hubris is my downfall

or maybe
it's my home after all

# clay

i was shaped
from air-dry clay
cracked
dusty
worn
but never fired

a relic on a shelf
an echo of
what might have been

i don't breathe
i don't eat
i don't sleep

a mindless existence

a hollow vessel
sitting
waiting
watching

never becoming more

## uneven

i am raw
mismatched
bashed
and beaten

i am too much
and too little
a little bit uneven

i am painted blue
and white
stripped
and burned

i am absence
words unsaid
a living
urn

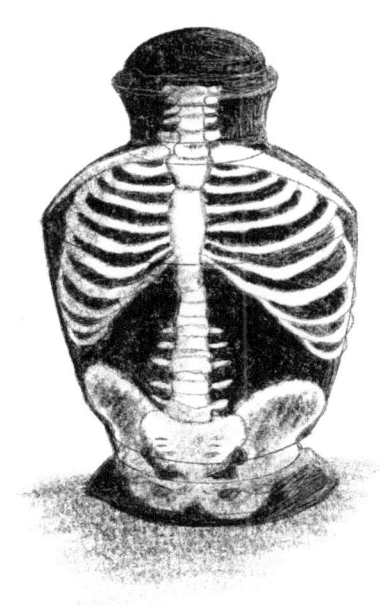

## termites

termites carve
elaborate holes
and tunnels
into their home

they eat at my mind
warping its walls
until i am left hollow
and a little dark inside

maybe they've eaten away
a bit too much
because
i don't mind anymore

at least
i am no longer alone

# chipped

i am the pause
between sentences
the space where meaning
goes to hide

i am the lamp
in a room no one enters
still lit
just in case

i am the chipped cup
on the highest shelf
not broken enough to toss
not wanted enough to use

i breathe
as if i might disappear
quietly
without complaint

*who would miss me*
*anyway?*

# laundromat

step inside my quiet laundromat
where rows of machines
hum secrets
spin memories
and swirl sorrow

the blue machine
dissolves the stains of grief
in cool
lifeless water
softening dark edges
until the fabric feels lighter
to hold

the red machine
spins anger clean
whirling fury into suds
scrubbing away the heat
until only soft warmth remains

the yellow machine
rinses fear
soothing trembling threads

until courage peeks through
fresh and bright as morning light

you drop your load in
and listen to the quiet whirl
as your clothes go round
and round

a gentle buzz signals it's ready
and a new cloth emerges
from the old

fresh with hope
ready to wear again

# moon child

i do not fear
or shake
or cry
or scream

i do not hope
or wish
or sleep
or dream

i do not wander
the world
unseen

instead
i stay numb
in my nimble cocoon
destined to be a hermit

a daughter of the moon

# otherworld

i do not wish
for food
or breath
they no longer sustain me

instead
i live my life
in books
and the worlds
beyond

# reflection

blank eyes
blink back at me

hair peppered
with grey

smile-less lips
weathered skin
a rounded face
an unfamiliar body

borrowed flesh
alien
and out of place

i don't recognise this person

i don't recognise me

i am a stranger
trapped behind glass

has time swapped my
reflection overnight?

*how*

how do i put it back
to what was?

## breathe

i breathe in
two
three
four

hold

out
two
three
four

the only thing i can do
to calm my racing mind

*that's what they say*

i anchor my breath to seconds
leaving everything else behind

but still
my thoughts run relentlessly

so i count
forevermore

# rope

*"how are you?"*
i am near the summit
of mount everest
the world lies small
beneath my feet
everything feels possible
and within my grasp
as i rise
from what tried
to break me

*"how are you?"*
i am sinking through silence
into the darkest depths
of the mariana trench
no light
no echo
just pressure and pulse
i cannot see
or hear
or speak

only the thud
of my lonely heart
keeps time
in the dark

*"how are you?"*
i am both
mountain and abyss
yin and yang
rise and fall
flesh and fog
i am opposite ends
of a tug of war
pulling apart
all at once

how is this possible?
is it because i am human?
and *this*
this is the fight
of being

## between

sharks circling
heart pounding
tears streaming
thoughts screaming

i'm teetering
on the edge
where up is down
and fear blurs
into reason

am i facing a breakdown
or a breakthrough?

they feel the same to me

# janitor

at 3:14 a.m.
i sighed
and sprouted wings

my veins peeled into rivers
my lungs called to oceans
my heart sang jazz to the moon

the janitor
dipped his mop in starlight
and swept the troubles of the day
from my mind

by dawn
it's all folded back
neat
forgetful
normal again

but the janitor
still smells the moon
on his overalls

# tea party

i set the table in the late afternoon
sunlight pooling
like honey on the tablecloth

fear arrives early
drenched in grey
carrying too much luggage
eyes darting
hands trembling
she says nothing
but sits anyway

hope is late as always
breezing in
with flower petals in her hair
dropping apologies and sugar cubes
as she takes her place

i pour the tea
watch the steam rise
and try to hold the silence
as it wobbles between us

fear stirs too fast
spills a little
says she's sorry for the mess
again and again

hope just smiles gently
dabs at the stain
and offers a slice of lemon cake

we sit like that for a while
sipping slowly
the three of us making room
at the same fragile table

# perspective

when i was a child
the world felt
limitless
and safe

now
as an adult
i see it's constrained
and often cruel

a constant battle of wills

some days are bright
most are dark

it takes strength to navigate
a world that's falling apart

## encroach

heatless flame
melting ice
bite-less wolf
crumbling stone
a crowd's pitchfork
for all to atone

a weeping sigh
a staggered fleet
a mountain goat
who's lost all sleep

an endless storm
a creeping vine
an encroach
on all
i hold
*divine*

## strings

the world curdles

the stench of sulphur
leached deep into our souls
and yet we do not notice

distracted by senseless noise
and politicians' lies
we breathe in toxic fumes
until we're spaced out
unaware
drifting through endless fog

they laugh at us
they sneer at
our blindness
while they control the stage

or so they think

but what is a puppet show
without an audience?
*meaningless*

what is a speech
without listening ears?
*meaningless*

what are they
without us?
*meaningless*

they hold the illusion of power
but *we*
we hold the strength
to cut the strings

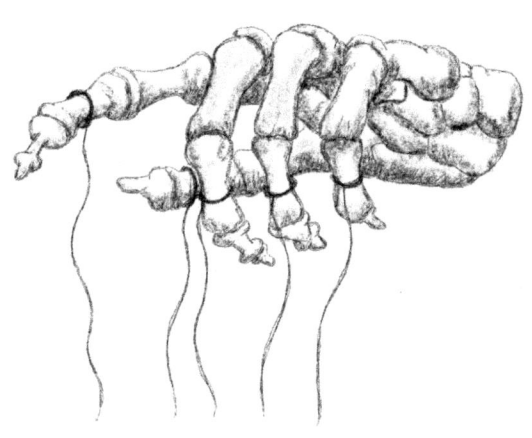

## you and me

i am stone
whittled bone
carved wood
iron throne

i am silk dresses
traded tea
seasonal balls
dancing with glee

i am welded
and processed
a concrete tree
a surge of data
pure electricity

i am time eternal
a sphere of us
a raging kaleidoscope
of everyone
before me

i am not singular
for we are all connected

there is no *i*
in *you* and *me*

# dreams

in my dreams
the night becomes a soft blanket

there is no rush
no sharp edges
only a quiet space
where i can breathe

my younger self
sits beside me
and we watch stars blink slowly
like they're winking secrets
just for us

no storms
only the gentle rhythm
of a heart finally at rest

i wake
carrying a flicker
of that quiet dark
woven softly beneath my skin
ready for the day

## thaw

the garden lies beneath
a heavy quiet
snow muffling every sound

roots hold their breath
waiting
for something softer

beneath the cold
life stirs
not yet spring
but no longer frozen

i am here broken
but not undone
it's time for my beginning

# quiet soles

sometimes
we have to learn
to keep walking
even when the ground
disappears

## morning sun

i lay in my void
a duvet cocoon
existing outside of space
and time

then the darkness
began to wane
as morning light flickered
soaking into the walls

i didn't move
but something in me softened

a thought
a breath
the faintest pull
towards living

# **echo**

your heartbeat
is the only sign of life
echoing into my
hollow chest

without you
i am a husk
a shell
a memory of what was

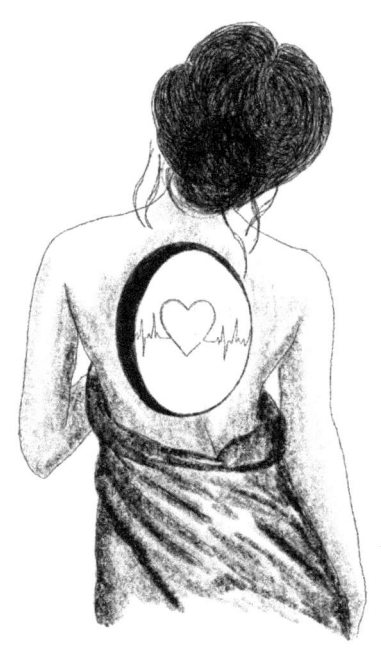

# hold me

hold me tight
do
not
let
go

if your fingers slip
i drift
too distant

for your touch
and breath
have become my own

without you
i cease to exist

# listen

my mind doesn't listen
to my calming thoughts
it calls them traitors
a trojan horse

my mind doesn't listen
to anyone's advice
it races and screams
trapped in its vice

my mind doesn't listen
to anyone
but you
your presence is my reason
you make me
anew

## colour

i lived in a grey world
with hollow words
and glass houses

now i see colour
promises have hold
and love creates a
home

i am irrevocably changed
since i met
you

# constant

your hand

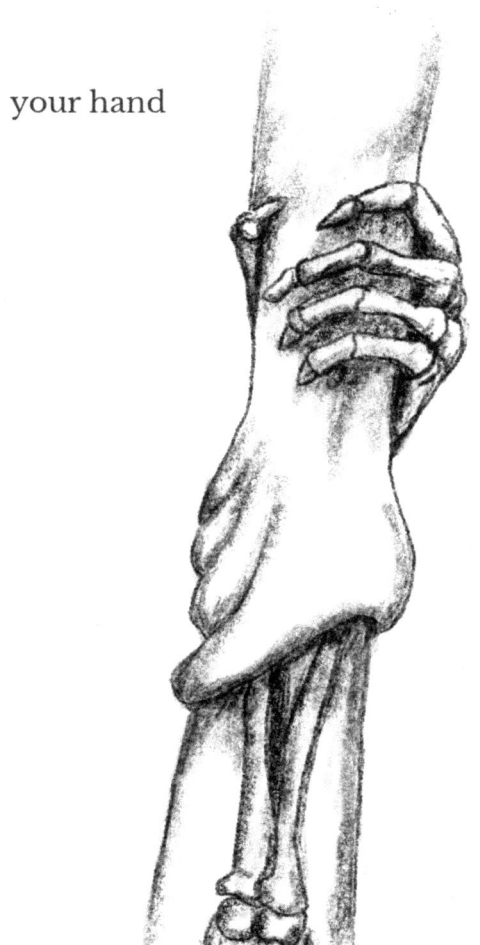

is the only
constant

in this
changing world

# solidarity

a soft wind carries the promise
that the storm will pass

that i'll find my way again

the trees rustle
sighing in relief beside me

i smile
just for a moment
not because i have the answers
but because i don't feel so alone

thank you
for the solidarity

# hibernation

i didn't sprout all at once
nor awaken right after hibernation

i emerged slowly
weary
a little broken

my fruits were not bountiful
at least
not at first

but as my leaves emerged
the first green shoots through frost
timid yet strong

i learned
there is beauty
in blooming
at your own pace

# fog

the fog came
slow and quiet
slipping in through the trees
and over the road
as if it had something to say

it settled on rooftops
and shoulders
hung low in the chest
and curled around thoughts
til they blurred at the edges

it stayed for days
maybe weeks
maybe longer
time softened inside it
like paper left out in the rain

and then
one morning
without reason or warning

the fog forgot
why it came

unfolded itself
from branches
from lungs
from the backs of our minds

and drifted off
as quietly as it arrived
like a question
that no longer needed
an answer

# shadow girl

i was the girl
afraid of my own shadow

the world seemed dark
menacing
with threats looming
that no one else could see

but then
i glimpsed sunlight
trees dipped in gold
birds singing
flying free

so i looked again

a passerby smiled
a baby laughed
a stranger said hello
she kindly spoke to me

i saw the light in the world
and realised
i am safer than i thought

and for the first time
in years
i stepped outside
*alone*

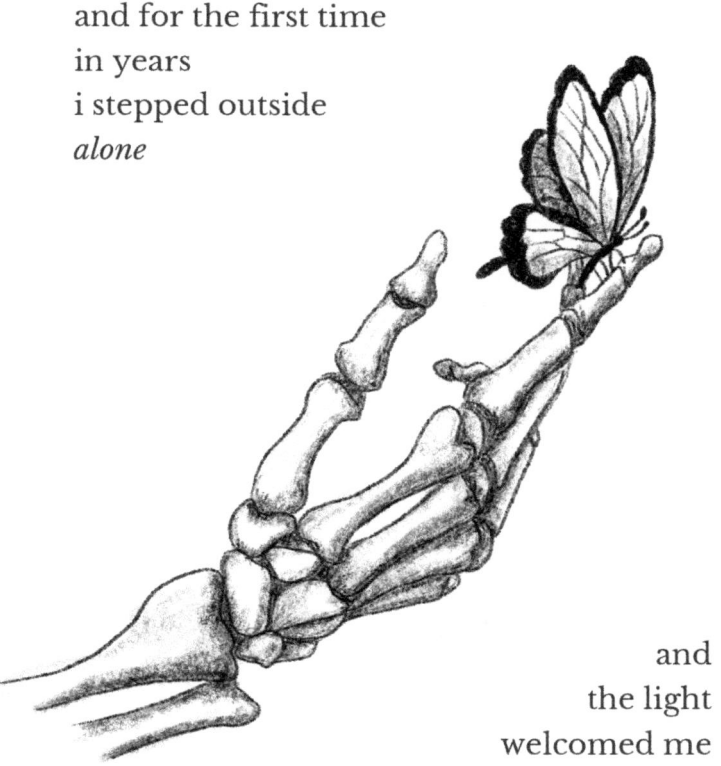

and
the light
welcomed me

## *i am more*

this is my body
my fingers
and toes
but i'm more than my looks
my shoes
and my clothes

i am my laughter
my thoughts
and my dreams
the questions i ask
and the plans
in between

i'm in my stories
the songs that i play
the way that i listen
and brighten a day

i'm how i feel things
sometimes too much

my kindness
my courage
my hope
and my touch

i'm my ideas
my voice when i speak
my quiet
my loud
my strong
and my weak

so see me as more
than the surface you view

because i am deeper
than you ever knew

# a reclaiming

i thought i was fragile
a whisper in a storm
shaken by every breath
dismantled by every glance

but beneath the quiet
a fire burned
smouldering
steady
waiting to roar

i gathered the shards
of who i was
piece by piece
and rebuilt my home

this body
my fortress
this mind
my blade

i am stronger
than i ever believed

and now
i reclaim
all that is mine

# fear

fear was my prisoner
my puppeteer
my deciding vote
my body's CEO
*my only friend*

she ruled my actions
my thoughts
my life
and everything i knew
*the entirety of me*

i was afraid to leave the house
afraid to be alone
listening to her
screaming inside
*that made everything die*

but then
i stopped

ignored
my quickening pulse

my raging lungs
my spiralling mind
*i can ride this wave*

she stripped me of my weapons
and begged me to bow
each time
i forgot who i was
*she became me*

but now i remember

i'm the queen of this body
the owner of this mind
the writer of this life
the winner of this war

i can feel fear
but it no longer stops me

i hugged her
and she
*crumbled*

# markers

i was 2D
line art
black and white
devoid of life

my heart begged
for colour
for vibrancy
for something more

i didn't realise
i held the markers
all along

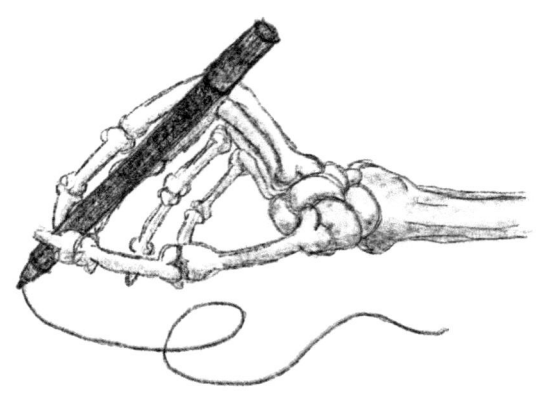

**now**

each heartbeat
is a gentle drum
reminding me
i'm here
i'm safe
and i am okay

i breathe slow
i hold still
letting the calm settle
deep within
my weary lungs

i am *now*

## power

my anxiety
used to ravage me
in a tornado
of what ifs
and devastation

with relentless
unforgiving power

until i realised
i had the power
to control the storm
to sway the tide
to hold the line

i had the power
to soothe
this unruly tempest
into tiny thoughts

# bloom

i planted seeds
inside my chest
quiet
small
waiting patiently
beneath the dark

sometimes
i forgot they were there
buried under old stones
and winter's long grey shadow

then one day
while resting
for the first time in a long while
i felt a soft stirring
a gentle yawn

and slowly
petal by petal
i began to bloom

# lonely moon

i was a lonely
little moon

cradled among flowers
in the frost

then the rain
whispered my name
and wrapped me
in its gentle arms

spring is here
my dear

it's time for you
to bloom

## richness

i find richness
in the small things now

the way sunlight scatters
through cracked windowpanes
dust shining like tiny stars

the weight of a warm cup
as bitter coffee
dances on my tongue

the soft murmur of trees
whispering secrets
only the wind understands

laughter bubbling up
unexpected
and free
like rain breaking a long drought

not lavish
or loud
but mine

# rise

i saw you
when you flinched
at nothing
when the world felt too loud
for your skin

you spoke softly
apologised for existing
folded yourself small
crushing the you within

but i also saw
the slow rebuilding
how you stitched yourself together
first with silence
then with strength

no grand speeches
no spotlight
just steady hands
and a will to go any length

now you stand
like the storm never touched you

but i remember
and i hope you do too

not to ache

but to see
how far
you've come

and to be proud
of all you do

through surviving
i unearthed life

through writing this book
i found my voice
and soul

now
i share my vulnerability
and fight
in the hope it helps you
with yours

# acknowledgments

thank you to those who held me,
believed in me,
or gave me the space to write.

and to the reader:
thank you for being here.

i hope these words walk beside you,
beyond this page.

# a gentle note

if this book has stirred difficult feelings,
please know you are not alone.

it's okay to take a moment.
to take care.
to reach out.

you might find it helpful to:
– reach out to trusted friends
– find local support groups or helplines
– speak with a mental health professional

there is support if you need it.

Freya O'Brien is an English poet and illustrator whose work explores the quiet, often unseen aspects of survival. Her writing moves through grief, chronic illness, trauma, and the quiet strength required to keep going.

She writes in fragments: during sleepless nights, in waiting rooms, and between breaths. Her poems serve as a form of witnessing for herself and for others who feel hollow, unravelled, or unseen.

*Hollow Bones* is her third collection and her most intimate to date, offering solace to those who have ever felt broken or unravelled.

You can find her on
Instagram: @by_freyaobrien
Website: www.freya-obrien.com

# More Books by Freya

If **Hollow Bones** felt like a friend,
you may find comfort in these pages too...

**Moon Child**
A relaxing and empowering poetry, colouring book for gentle souls.
Let your inner child come out to play.

**Lonely Lines**
A poetry collection for the aching heart.
Lonely Lines speaks to the parts of us that long to be seen, heard, and held.

Available from Amazon, Freya's website, and other booksellers.

thank you for reading

www.ingramcontent.com/pod-product-compliance
Lightning Source LLC
Chambersburg PA
CBHW061208070526
44583CB00025B/3160